AN ILLUSTRATED
HISTORY OF
ROAD
TANKERS

AN ILLUSTRATED HISTORY OF
ROAD TANKERS

HINTON J. SHERYN

Ian Allan PUBLISHING

CONTENTS

Front cover:
An ERF ES8 chassis with a unique front and rear-wheel steering system which must be good news when trying to deliver Calor Gas from this tanker into a narrow leafy driveway in those surban conurbations. *ERF and Calor Gas*

Back cover:
The Dennis Pax is being fuelled from his big brother the Dennis Max. Both are fitted with 1,000 gallon tanks for transportating tar, 2 August 1947. *Ian Allan Library*

Back cover bottom:
A self-propelled aviation lubricating oil dispenser built at Bilston by Thompson. *Ernie Flavell, Heil Trailer International*

Half Title:
An AEC with Park Royal cab loading with chemicals on 4 September 1965. *Ian Allan Library*

Title page:
The late 1930s/early 1940s would have set the scene for these Bedford road tankers. *Dennis Sherer, Vauxhall Motors*

CREDITS AND ACKNOWLEDGEMENTS

I would like to thank all of the following for their help with the making of this book:

Ian Allan Library
Tony Brown, St Helens
Keith Brown (Massey Tankers, Clitheroe, Lancashire)
Ken Dowding, Fruehauf of Dereham, Norfolk
Hannah Field (National Dairy Council)
Julian Fishwick, CEng (Whale Tankers, Solihull)
Ernie Flavell (Heil Trailer International, UK — formerly Thompson's, Thompson Carmichael, Thompson-Heil of Bilston)
Alison Hall (ERF Ltd)
Michele Harris (Heil Trailer International, USA)
Marny Hayward (Stiller Group)
Thomas Jennings, Phoenix Bitumen and Tar Tankers (Phoenix Engineering Co Ltd)
Carl J. Johnson (Register of ERF Vehicles Society)
Mick Johnson (S. J. Bargh Ltd)
Trevor Longcroft (ERF Ltd)
Peter Norfolk (Hazardous Cargo Bulletin)
Peter Norris (Clayton Commercials Ltd)
Jacqueline Numan (Bulk Distributor)
Elizabeth O'Connor (Peter Sawell & Partners Ltd)
J. A. Ostle and Sue McGoldrick (BOC Gases)
Mavis Pearson
Anna Peyron (Scania Image Desk)
Dez Rigg and all at Washington Hall, Chorley
Cheryl Saponia (Petroleum Review)
Dennis Sherer (Vauxhall Heritage Centre)
Michael Sutton and Miss Paula Bradley (Sutton's Transport)
Bernard Titcombe (Kew Bridge Steam Museum)
Vivian-Tove Breihahn (Hoyer GmbH)
The late R. L. Wilson (Wirral)

Photographs of GUINNESS-branded tankers provided by the Guinness Archive, Park Royal, London, with thanks to Sue Garland at the Guinness Archive and Guinness Limited, © Guinness Limited. All rights reserved.

I am also grateful to all companies whose names appear on photographs of the vehicles, or in the vicinity of the vehicles, and to all those who have helped in any way, whether mentioned or not.

First published 2001

ISBN 0 7110 2819 2

Published by Ian Allan Publishing

an imprint of Ian Allan Publishing Ltd, Hersham, Surrey KT12 4RG.
Printed by Ian Allan Printing Ltd, Hersham, Surrey KT12 4RG.

Code: 0111/B

INTRODUCTION

For much of the early 19th century only the horse-drawn tanker or 'bowser' was in use for the transportation of liquids, most of which were sewage sludge or water. As early as 1828 a horse-drawn water tank, complete with a scraper and a fixed brush made from heather, was patented by Messrs Boase and Smith of London. This, though, was used for street cleaning.

From the late 19th century hundreds of steam traction engines and steam rollers were being made by companies such as Garrett, Ransomes, Sims & Jeffries, John Fowler, Robey, Clayton and Shuttleworth, Burrell, Rushton & Hornsby, Aveling & Porter, Armstrong Whitworth, Collings and Brown & May. All of these needed large volumes of water which would be converted into steam, so the requirement for transporting water was pressing. By this time there were also hundreds of steam-powered cranes and excavators in use, often working in remote parts of the world at mines and quarries, and helping to build railways, dams, canals and, indeed, the early infrastructure of our towns and cities today. These too required water carts. Another use for early mobile tanks was the transportation of bitumen for the (then) new-fangled paved or tarred road surface.

Engines and machinery which were in constant motion simply would not function without lubrication. Lubricating oils have for many years been distributed in steel drums, as has tar, but where vast amounts of oil were required to keep machinery working, then only bulk deliveries by road tankers would suffice.

Milk was another liquid which was first transported in horse-drawn bulk tankers before motorised vehicles took over. Although wooden and then steel milk churns were used for very many years to take milk from the farm gate to dairies, the bulk milk tanker played a very important part in the movement of large volumes of milk over great distances to cheese factories, butter manufacturers and milk distribution centres. Breweries, too, have been using bulk road tankers from the early years of the 20th century.

Gases for industrial, commercial, domestic and, not least, medical use have, again, been moved by bulk tankers for very many years. Vehicles which transport highly inflammable, toxic or hazardous materials by road have been subject to strict legislation from as far back as the Explosives Act of 1875 and orders made under the Petroleum (Consolidation) Act of 1928 as well as legislation specifically relating to carbon disulphate. From 1970, however, the laws relating to the transportation and not least to the labelling of chemicals have become very much more rigid. The words 'Poison' and 'Highly Inflammable' are a regular feature of the decor of modern-day bulk road tankers. The symbols used help the emergency services identify a dangerous chemical or substance, enabling them (and in particular the fire brigades) to know just how to approach the material.

Right:
Many manufacturers on both sides of the Atlantic were builders of horse-drawn tankers. They were made to carry a variety of liquids, including oil products, tar, water, milk and beers. One company manufactured water carts from before 1905, when the reproduced advertisements featured here were listed in their catalogue, along with many implements for use by municipal authorities, contractors and builders. These included hand-operated rollers, wheelbarrow-mounted water and sludge pumps, fire baskets (for watchmen), heating stoves, mastic and asphalt boilers and cauldrons and hand-operated derrick cranes and shear legs. Since those days, The Phoenix Engineering Co of Chard, Somerset have been kept very busy producing lorry-mounted tar tanks and tar spreaders. The 1905 Phoenix Engineering Co catalogure shows a Model 'C' pattern street-watering and flushing van drawn by horses. The range included those from 300 gallons capacity to 450 gallons. *Phoenix Bitumen and Tar Tankers (Phoenix Engineering Co Ltd)*

The United Nations Committee of Experts developed a system in 1975 whereby substances in a particular class or division are divided into three groups according to the degree of danger they present when transported. They are:

Group I   Very dangerous substances
Group II   Substances presenting medium danger
Group III Substances presenting minor danger

The United Nations Economic and Social Council had already accepted recommendations made by the Committee of Experts of the United Nations in 1957 for the classification, definition, listing, packing, labelling and documentation of dangerous goods. It took a further 12 years of painstaking work undertaken by the Committee of Experts before final publication of *Transport of Dangerous Goods*. This publication lists all 'Dangerous Goods Most Commonly Carried' and it is referred to as 'The Orange Book'.

No such list can be exhaustive, and therefore the List of Dangerous Goods includes 'NOS entries', ie references to groups of substances which are 'not otherwise specified' by name. The main UN classes and divisions are:

Above:
The Phoenix Model 'D' pattern was an improved version of the horse-drawn water wagons and was of the same capacity as the Model 'C'. *Phoenix Bitumen and Tar Tankers (Phoenix Engineering Co Ltd)*

Class 1   Explosives

Class 2   Gases
  Division 2.1 Flammable gases
  Division 2.2 Non-flammable, compressed gases
  Division 2.3 Toxic gases

Class 3   Flammable liquids

Class 4   Flammable solids
  Division 4.1 Flammable solids. Solids, other than those classed as explosives which, under conditions encountered in transport, are readily combustible or may cause or contribute to fire through friction.
  Division 4.2 Substances liable to spontaneous combustion. Substances which are liable to spontaneous heating under normal conditions encountered in transport, or to heating up in contact with air and being liable to catch fire.
  Division 4.3 Substances which, in contact with water, emit flammable gases. Substances which, in interaction with water, are liable to become spontaneously inflammable or to give off flammable gases in dangerous quantities. (One such chemical, known as Hydros, once caused a major fire on an articulated flat-bed trailer at a West Country china clay works during the late 1960s because the driver did not cover the bags with a tarpaulin sheet and overnight rain caused the Hydros to get wet and to ignite.) Certain fertilizers are particularly at risk from explosion or fire if wet.

Class 5   Oxidising substances; organic peroxides.
  Division 5.1 Oxidising substances other than organic peroxides.
  Division 5.2 Organic peroxides.

Class 6   Toxic and infectious substances.
  Division 6.1 Toxic substances.
  Division 6.2 Infectious substances containing disease-producing micro-organisms.

Class 7   Radioactive material.

Class 8   Corrosive substances.

Class 9   Miscellaneous dangerous substances (substances which, during transport, present a danger not covered by other classes; for example, hot liquids such as tar).

The Voluntary Tanker Marking Scheme was set up after a number of serious incidents drew attention to the lack of information for the emergency services. In 1972 a working party was formed, consisting of members from London Fire Brigade, the Chemical Industries Association, the Police and other interested bodies. A tanker marking scheme was developed, the essence of which lay in the display of a placard containing not only the Warning Diamond, but also three other vital pieces of information:

(a) A simple code was devised to indicate to the emergency services the immediate action to be taken in the event of a fire or spillage.

(b) The substance was identified by means of a Substance Identification Number allowing further information to be obtained from Brigade Control regarding the chemical, so that the incident could be cleared and rendered safe.

(c) In some cases specialist advice is needed and the ability to call for replacement vehicles is an advantage. Thus, a telephone number from which such facilities can be obtained whilst the tanker is in transit became part of the placard.

A pilot scheme combining the elements outlined above was introduced during 1974 in Cleveland, which attracted such favourable comment that in July 1975 it was promoted on a national scale, albeit voluntarily, and extended to cover a much wider range of substances.

The Hazardous Substances (Labelling of Road Tankers) Regulations 1978, which came into force in March 1979, converted the voluntary scheme into a mandatory one. These regulations have since been superseded by the Road Traffic (Carriage of Dangerous Substances in Road Tanker and Tank Containers) Regulations in force today. These regulations, together with the 'Approved List', form the basis of legislation covering the transport of hazardous materials in road tankers.

The list of serious potential accidents involving road tankers can be quite alarming. Happily, with the vehicles' meticulous design and construction, together with the important labelling system, major incidents are very rare indeed. However, in Spain, during the late 1960s, a road tanker transporting a Calor gas tank exploded in a village, causing a major catastrophe for the residents and emergency services alike. On another occasion in Mexico, a road tanker imploded (that is when the tank buckles inward), compressing the substances to such an extent that an almighty explosion was caused, described at the time as being reminiscent of an atomic bomb.

Protests in the mid-1960s from inhabitants of a small south Dartmoor village, which included the lobbying of all councillors (parish, district and county) and the local Member of Parliament, about a large Calor gas road tanker passing through the narrow streets of the village on its way to china clay plants twice every week, resulted in a total ban on this and

Above:
The Phoenix Model 'A' pattern was a range of water carts for use with horses. It had capacities of 75 to 200 gallons. *Phoenix Bitumen and Tar Tankers (Phoenix Engineering Co Ltd)*

other similar vehicles from using the shortened route through the village, due to fears of a major incident in the centre of the village. The Calor gas was being used as the main source of fuel for the large kilns required in the clay-drying process by the company.

Daily, all manner of materials, including chemicals, are transported by road and rail across the world. Indeed, china clay is now transported predominantly by bulk tankers, as are cement, stone dust, limestone dust, dyes for paint, ceramics, cloth. So too are fertilizers, pesticides, cobalt, thousands of chemicals from liquids, solids and gases, water, beer, oil, diesel, petrol, tar, corn, wheat, maize, rice, sugar, salt to a whole host of foodstuffs and edible products such as cooking oils, milk and dairy products, as well as used oils (for recycling) and the less pleasant substances such as sewage sludge and radioac-

Below:
The Phoenix Model 'B' pattern ranged from 200–300 gallon capacity and differed from the earlier model in having heavy-duty springs installed. *Phoenix Bitumen and Tar Tankers (Phoenix Engineering Co Ltd)*

7

tive material (though these are often carried in specially designed and built heavy-duty flasks or tanks, able to withstand abnormal impact in an incident — though even these have been known to fail tests).

Ironically, in August and September of 2000, the importance of road tanker haulage, which had perhaps gone largely ignored, was felt in countries right across Europe, including Great Britain, when farmers, hauliers and the general public protested vigorously at high oil prices and equally high taxes on fuel. During the blockade of the oil refineries in Great Britain, the thousands of petrol stations in the country realised that they were going to run out of supplies of fuel in less than a week as panic buying by motorists added to the problem. For a week or more tankers were prevented from leaving refineries such as Stanlow in Cheshire, except for deliveries to enable the emergency services and hospitals to keep going, even though these too were suffering because key staff were finding it difficult to jump the very long queues at stations where a nominal amount of fuel was still available.

Once the blockades had ended and the tankers were again back on the roads, often convoys of as many as 10, 12, 16 or even 20 vehicles were leaving the refineries in an effort to replenish the fuel stations so that the country could start returning to some sort of normality. Government ministers, heads of police, oil companies, tanker operators, union officials and other interested bodies have been forced to draw up measures which will prevent such restrictions or hindrances to the movement of fuel if any subsequent protests should occur.

The future of road tankers is assured as progress in a modern world continues. Where fuel is required, whether it is gas, petrol, diesel, paraffin, kerosene, pulverised coal or the related lubricating fluids, the road tanker will play a vital part in society. Millions upon millions of gallons of petrol and diesel for automobiles is required throughout the world on a daily basis. In addition, the requirements of buses, railway engines (where electrification is not an option), hauliers, agricultural tractor and machinery operators, construction, demolition, mining and quarrying opera-

One of Thompson's very early products was this horse-drawn road tanker from around 1904–06.
Ernie Flavell, Heil Trailer International

9

Above:
A tank trailer destined for military use and made by Thompson. *Ernie Flavell, Heil Trailer International*

tions (where very large dump-trucks, bulldozers, excavators, etc can swallow 30 or more gallons of fuel an hour), aircraft, boats and ships of every conceivable size, rockets, and fuel for the heating of homes, hospitals, schools, shops and factories, where it is not piped direct to the facility, will all require millions of journeys by road for the tankers to keep a modern economy going.

What about times of armed conflict? Tanks, aircraft, landing craft, armoured vehicles, support vehicles, ambulances and large ships will always require fuel. In the remote desert or jungle, or in urban conflicts, where vehicles are required to reach the front line of attack or defence, fuel must get through at all costs.

The food producing industries are again a very vital service. So much raw material and finished product is now transported using road tankers that without these vehicles, food shortages would become inevitable. Cattle, sheep, pigs and poultry all depend on bulk tankers to deliver their food or replenish the silos, whilst arable farms rely on tankers to supply seed, fertilizer, pesticides and organic products to assist crop growth. The end product is likely to be removed from the farms to the flour mills and bakeries by bulk tanker. Further foodstuffs such as chocolate and its ingredients are also transported by road tankers.

The construction of bulk tanks is of vital concern for operators and the public alike. For example, a tank

with a total capacity of 30,000 litres, but which is carrying only half or three-quarters of that amount of liquid, would run the severe risk of the load moving to and fro at a rapid rate within the tank as the vehicle speeds along the highway. When the driver is forced to apply the brakes to avoid an oncoming emergency situation (ie the build-up of traffic, traffic signals, narrow lanes, bridges, roadworks, wide loads or other obstacles), the load could slop about internally with such force as to potentially cause a serious accident. The vehicle could perhaps jack-knife (when the articulated trailer appears alongside the tractor unit), or the moving load could force the tractor and trailer through the braking system, at the least causing untold damage to the gearbox. To prevent such problems tankers are often 'bunded', ie the tank is separated into compartments, so that smaller amounts of liquid are allowed free movement than would otherwise by the case.

Where foodstuffs, edible liquids and biorganic materials (crop seeds) are carried, cleanliness of the internal structure of the tanks is of prime importance. That is why so many tankers are constructed of stainless steels, carbon steels and aluminium (which also reduces the gross vehicle weight [gvw] of the vehicle).

Imagine the problems which would be caused if little or no attention was paid to the thorough cleaning, washing, disinfecting and rinsing of tankers which regularly carry milk, chocolate or other dairy products — or beers, lagers or other alcoholic or non-alcoholic drinks. E. coli or other notoriously dangerous bacteria could be the cause of sickness or even death on an unprecedented scale. What, too, if a tanker used to carry genetically modified seeds had not been thoroughly

The rear end of a road tanker from 1920.
The tank was built by Thompson Brothers.
Ernie Flavell, Heil Trailer International

Above:

This Thompson tank was fitted to an articulated trailer by Dyson sometime in the early 1930s. *Ian Allan Library*

Below:

This Fordson was fitted with Eagle 'ARP & Municipal' tank and equipment. *Ian Allan Library*

cleaned out before being used to transport a load containing non-genetically modified seeds, and the second load cross-pollinated with, perhaps, unforeseen disastrous results? It is for these reasons that the bulk tanker road haulage industry is not only very well regulated but also the manufacturers, operators and owners of such vehicles are highly professional and the drivers themselves are subjected to vigorous training sessions. The drivers of fuel tankers are amongst the most highly trained and skilled operators of land-based vehicles anywhere on earth. Their responsibility for prompt delivery times, coupled with hazardous driving conditions in all types of weather (fog, snow, ice, heavy rain,

A Thornycroft Trusty articulated bulk tanker dating from 1939. *Ian Allan Library*

gales or even the other extremes — heat, dust, sand-storms or flash lightening) and their ability to negotiate a long articulated tanker lorry through busy traffic-congested streets of towns, cities or just small villages to reach filling stations in the middle of built-up areas calls for discipline that would be hard to find in most drivers of motor vehicles in our fast and busy world.

For many years, back into the horse-drawn tanker days, it would have been possible to witness two or even three tanks being hauled by the same team of horses, even though it is likely additional horses would be deployed to add much-needed muscle to the heavy work. Subsequently, rigid-chassis engine-powered road vehicles at times were used to tow a trailer tank behind the lorries' own chassis-borne tank and today large-capacity articulated road tankers have been spotted with two, three or four tanks being hauled by the same tractor unit. In Australia, Mack Titans powered by mighty 600hp Cummins diesel engines are employed to haul four — yes, four! — tanks containing a total of 128,000 litres (157 tonnes gvw) of diesel fuel for use in far-flung opencast mines, in which many of the world's largest-capacity dump trucks (currently standing at

around 340 tons) and associated equipment such as large hydraulic excavators, bulldozers, graders and scrapers, wheel loaders, etc are being used in the extraction of gold, copper, iron ore, diamonds or coal. Other users of fuel brought by these huge road trains are farmers and ranchers at the cattle stations in the Australian outback. With a round trip of nearly 3,000 kilometres from the refinery at Darwin to places as remote as Alice Springs, it does make sense to reduce the number of trips to be made by one fuel tanker, or at least to enable the tanker to take a full-capacity load.

The manufacture of highly specialised forms of material transporters, such as road tankers, requires technical skills not associated with other forms of transport. For example, the production of tanks with several compartments, each with precise capacities for gases, liquids, powders or other products, requires very careful calculation so that by the time the testing stage is reached the capacity fits the specifications required. This can be particularly difficult with certain liquids which also produce noxious gases or fumes — petrol, for example — so an allowance must be made for the volume of both the liquid and gas. Special valves are installed which can remove the gases or fumes, while in modern tankers all compartments are fitted with their own capacity meters. No longer will you see a man on top of a tanker using a long metal dipstick to ascertain how much liquid is in the tank.

Above:
Thompson built this streamlined tanker fitted to a Bedford chassis, for aircraft refuelling service in 1939/40. *Ian Allan Library*

Below:
One of a batch of six Thornycroft Trusty 6 x 4 normal-control left-hand-drive chassis equipped with all-steel insulated cabs and 2,500-gallon water, petrol and oil tanks. These vehicles were ordered by the Kuwait Oil Co Ltd for shipment to the Middle East. The tanks were manufactured by the Steel Barrel Company of Uxbridge, Middlesex. At the rear of each vehicle a sprinkler bar was fitted so that the duty of road sprinkling could be carried out as an occasional requirement. This view dates from c1955/6. *Ian Allan Library*

With CAD (Computer-Aided Design), the tanker is designed by highly skilled engineers using the latest computer technology. The software used on the computer-controlled cutting machine on the factory shop floor enables the exact dimensions of the stainless steel or aluminium sheets to be cut which will form the convex ends to the tank, the inner compartment separation walls and the main tank walls. All of these are then put together with strips and automatically welded. Hatchways, valves, pipe fittings and other important accessories are integrated into the design from the original design software. Careful attention has to be paid to the overall trailer design. Will it be built into a rigid chassis, two-axle articulated trailer, or three-axle unit? Will free-standing support legs be included to enable the tank to stand free of the tractor unit? Will the fifth wheel (hitch point) be long enough to effect an adequate turning radius of articulation with whatever combination of axle the trailer will feature?

Often, the skills to produce such complex tankers have come only with the experience of many years, if not decades, of production and a knowledge of the changes in design which have occurred over such long periods. Many such modifications have been brought about not only to increase the capacity of the vehicles but also to bring them into line with the international laws, rules and regulations governing the road (and rail) transportation of toxic, inflammable or dangerous substances, as mentioned earlier in the Introduction.

Another important milestone in the development of road tankers is the use over a number of years of tanker heating systems, particularly for vehicles which transport such substances as tar and bitumen products which have to be kept at a specific temperature to prevent clogging or sticking to the internal compartment walls or baffles. These innovations might take the form of hot water circulated through pipes or electrically heated bars contained in metal tubes, and in both these cases may be powered by the main engine on the tractor unit

Below:
An Albion Clydesdale chassis fitted with a 1,900-gallon stainless steel tank, one of a fleet of Leyland Group vehicles operated by Peter Tennant of Forth, Lanarkshire. The tank was constructed by Associated Metal Works (Glasgow) Limited and mounted on the chassis by ABM Tulloch Ltd of Glasgow. The vehicle was engaged in the transport of milk throughout Lanarkshire and Midlothian in Scotland during the 1960s and 1970s.
Ian Allan Library

Above:

Sutton's is currently one of the biggest haulage companies in the UK, with a section totally devoted to tanker transport. The company headquarters is in St Helens, with a major tanker depot in Widnes, Cheshire. This is just one of its earlier articulated road tankers using an Atkinson tractor. Almost all of its tanker-trailers are built by Clayton Commercials of Burscough, near Wigan.

Michael Sutton/Sutton Transport

Below:

A Clayton tri-axle tanker behind one of Sutton Transport's Foden 4320 tractors.

Tony Brown/Sutton Transport

Above:
A typical 1980s–mid-1990s cryogenic tanker consisting of a barrel of alloy inner and outer skin, with stainless steel pipework.
J. A. Ostle / Sue McGoldrick, BOC Gases

or truck, or by means of a separate engine fitted to the tanker trailer. The high cost of the latter would normally ensure that the tanker is used specifically for one purpose, for example bitumen products.

The cleaning of internal compartments of a bulk tanker has to be uppermost in the minds of operators who regularly transport foodstuffs such as milk, chocolate or flour. Likewise, the transportation of cement, tar products, stone dust or other powder products such as china clay or calcium carbonates has to adhere to a strict guideline of regular and thorough cleaning. This is often carried out by companies who specialise only in the cleaning of bulk tankers, using high-pressure hot water and detergent sprinkler systems which are operated from the man-entry facilities at the top of the tanks.

The loading and emptying of bulk tankers can vary according to the types of substances carried. Gases and liquid petroleum products are pumped on board via hoses, with all the accuracy that state-of-the-art measuring devices can provide. They are often emptied in the same way. Tankers hauling powdered products have to utilise specially designed internal features, for instance to chill egg products at 4°C plus or minus ½°C, to ensure the maximum discharge of all substances from the tank without clogging exit channels.

Certain products require to be kept at below a maximum temperature so some bulk tankers need heating/refrigeration systems. Milk and chocolate are two examples of food substances which are normally subject to refrigeration to prevent 'splitting' (ie butterfats separating from the rest of the milk, or ingredients of liquid chocolate from separating, as can happen if it is not kept below 45°C.) Certain chemicals need to be kept at very low temperatures to control any possibility of a reaction.

The capacity of current road tankers does vary according to need, but can be from as little as 1,000 litres to 55,000 litres under current legislation. New laws allowing road tankers to operate up to 44 tonnes gross vehicle weight are expected to come into force in the UK by 2003. This will increase the tanker's load-carrying capacity, often enabling it to travel greater distances with its cargo and operate more economically. This could bring about a reduction in the numbers of tankers on the road and almost certainly a reduction in the amount of chemicals, gas or foodstuffs currently being transported by rail. However, 44-tonne gvw vehicles are already operating on the roads of the United Kingdom, provided the road journey is broken for part of the distance by the tanker being transported by rail. The current standard gvw, as at 2000/2001, is 38-tonnes, which has remained the same for some years. The additional weights anticipated on our roads in the future is the reason why a massive programme of bridge strengthening has been taking place, to help roads (and bridges in particular) to cope with the increased pounding from much heavier vehicles than they were originally designed for.

Above:
King Tanktechnic Ltd offers a specialist service to oil companies to maintain their petroleum facilities, installing, testing, cleaning and inspecting tanks, transferring fuel, decommissioning sites, etc. Shown behind a Scania 93m chassis unit is a King Tanktechnic tank service unit. The three-compartment vacuum tanker carries full personnel safety apparatus, testing and engineering maintenance equipment and is fitted with integral equipment for water jetting, product transfer and compressed air tools.
King Tanktechnic Ltd

Below:
An ERF articulated road tanker from Thompson with an Albion/Thompson Brothers tank of a very much earlier vintage. This little Albion is still well preserved at the Thompson factory, now Heil Trailer International, UK at Bilston.
Ernie Flavell, Heil Trailer International

Illustrated History of ROAD TANKERS

Precursors to road tankers were the early horse-drawn water carts manufactured by companies such as The Bristol Wagon and Carriage Works Ltd, whose other vehicles included dust wagons (see the author's previous book *An Illustrated History of Dustcarts*, published by Ian Allan Publishing, 2000), ambulances, disinfecting vans and carts. These were also made available as motorised vehicles.

John Smith and Sons of Inkermann Street, Wolverhampton, and Pritchett Street in Birmingham, had been building horse-drawn water carts, tumbler carts, sweeping machines and tipping carts and vans for municipal and commercial work since 1794.

The Caink's patent sprinklers were built into watering and flushing carts and vans by Maldon Iron Works Co Ltd of Maldon, Essex, from the middle of the 19th century. All of the company's vehicles were of the horse-drawn type. However, companies such as Manns, Leyland, J. Thornycroft, Karrier, Guy and Foden, and many others, began building either steam- or petrol-powered tankers from the end of the 19th century. Alongside these now famous names were others equally well known from abroad including Puch (a part of the Austro-Daimler Co), Benz, Mack Brothers (United States), Orion (of Switzerland), and so on. However, many of the companies who built the chassis of these vehicles did not always produce the tanks they carried. Often that task was left to tank-manufacturing specialists and engineering companies such as Thompson's of Bilston.

Right:

When the horse was the usual form of power for the transportation of goods, tankers were included as a means of moving liquids such as oil, water and beer. Here we see a 2 horse power bulk tanker being used to transport oil. Tanks such as these had a capacity of between 1000-3600 litres. The fact that Germany was the home of the first petroleum-fuelled car makes it likely that many such tankers descended from mainland Europe, with America and Canada coming a fairly close second. *Catherine Cosgrove and Cheryl Saponia, Petroleum Review/Michael Wood*

Transporting blue oil from Drohobycz refinery to Boryslaw refinery for use as fuel, Galacia in 1903. *Catherine Cosgrove and Cheryl Saponia, Petroleum Review/Michael Wood*

Merryweather

The Merryweather company began making hoses and horse-drawn carts from as early as 1797, and very possibly before that. At first, most of its products were used for the removal of sewage from cesspools and crude street gullies. It was soon realised, however, that these horse-drawn carts and the hoses they carried with them could be put to other uses, particularly as fire appliances, for which Merryweather has long been a famous name. Over time, these road tankers and their accessories found a growing market throughout the United Kingdom, and a vast market existed abroad also. By the 20th century the company was producing horse-drawn carts alongside steam and petrol-driven road tankers, many for use in Great Britain, while others were ordered for work all over the world — Spain, Demerara in South America, South Africa and Ireland being just some of the places.

Merryweather & Sons Ltd from Greenwich Road in south east London and Long Acre WC, produced a range of horse-drawn vacuum water tankers, mainly for the exhausting of cesspools. The apparatus featured here was being advertised in the company's literature during the 1890s.
Author's collection

Right:
Los Angeles oilfield around 1908. The oil is being drawn from the storage tank by gravity feed into a horse-drawn road tanker — a familiar vehicle for this period. *Catherine Cosgrove and Cheryl Saponia, Petroleum Review/Michael Wood*

Main:
In Russia, too, liquefied fuel was being refined at an alarming rate by the turn of the century. Here we see fuel for use in boilers being drawn off from field storage tanks and loaded into a horse-drawn tank wagon at Suvorov in 1901. *Catherine Cosgrove and Cheryl Saponia, Petroleum Review/Michael Wood*

Back at the turn of the century this Wisconsin-built ... Wisconsin-built ... ... transport tan... ... ... of K... delivery of kerosene and gasoline by the bucket.... THE HEIL co

Above:
This horse-drawn tanker trailer was built by the Heil Company at its Wisconsin factory around the turn of the century (1900) for the delivery of kerosene and gasoline which was handed out, literally, by the bucket load.
Michele Harris, Heil Trailer International

Below:
In 1914 Heil designed and built the first electrically-welded compartment tanks. The one shown had four individual compartments. *Michele Harris, Heil Trailer International*

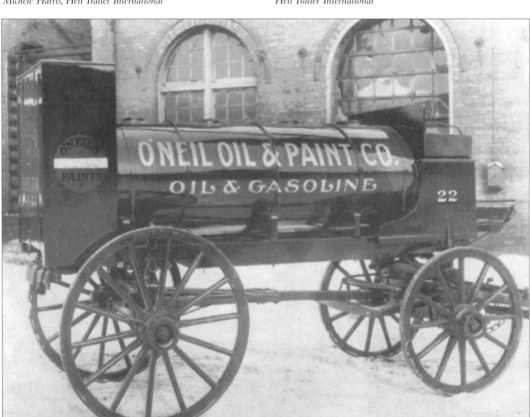

O'NEIL OIL & PAINT CO.
OIL & GASOLINE
22

Above:
A 1916 water tank produced for the US Army by Heil and mounted on a four-wheel-drive truck. The tanks were used by General John Pershing's troops in the Mexican Border Campaign when pursuing Pancho Villa through the wilds of Northern Mexico. These were among the first electrically-welded tanks and proved far superior to riveted tanks in this particularly gruelling test. *Michele Harris, Heil Trailer International*

Right:
From the Swedish firm Scania we have a 3-tonner complete with petroleum tank; this vehicle was delivered to the operator in March 1915. *Anna Peyron, Scania Image Desk*

Top:
In operation in 1910 was this Vabis F4 engine
¼-tonner, working in Gothenburg, Sweden.
Anna Peyron, Scania Image Desk

Above:
Scania delivered this type Dla tanker in February
1920. *Anna Peyron, Scania Image Desk*

24

Above:

From the Gilford Motor Co we have this road tanker in the livery of Dominion Oils. The picture is dated 2 July 1931. *Ian Allan Library*

Below:

An unusual articulation is to be seen on this 1932 Bedford tanker. *Ian Allan Library*

Bottom:

A Bussing road tanker at work in London on the 27 July 1929 with M. & W. Mack. *Ian Allan Library*

Top:
**Tankers ready for action at Thompson Brothers'
Bilston factory. All are thought to be Morris–
Commercials and ADCs from the 1920s.**
Ernie Flavell, Heil Trailer International

Above:
An early 1930s AEC road tanker. *Ian Allan Library*

Above:
This AEC Ranger is fitted with a Butterfields tank to haul glucose for the Albion Sugar Co of Woolwich in London. The picture is dated 5 December 1936. *Ian Allan Library*

Below:
Collecting and delivering milk in New South Wales, Australia, on 28 March 1936 was this Albion road tanker. *Ian Allan Library*

Above:
Thompson tanks mounted on Leyland chassis ready for work in the early 1920s.
Ernie Flavell, Heil Trailer International

Thompson

The founder of this world-renowned engineering company was William Thompson (1814-78). William established himself as a boilermaker in 1834, after having worked in his father's coal mine from the age of 10 and then two years later beginning an apprenticeship at G. B. Thornycroft of Bilston, Staffordshire, already a well-known name in boiler making. (Strangely enough, at that time the area around Wolverhampton was better known for wool than for the engineering in which it made its name during the reign of Queen Victoria and beyond.)

In 1840 (the year his second son, John, was born) William Thompson set up a business at the Manor Works at Highfields. Brilliant though he was at designing and building boilers and other engineered products, his business sense was exploited by competitors on a fairly regular basis. The lack of patents on his designs and the deep economic depression of the time created enormous problems for the company. Eventually the business was taken over by William's younger brother, Stephen, whose drive and enthusiasm, and business-like approach, were able to create a solid foundation to hand on to William's son, John. The boilermaking business moved to new premises at Ettingshall adjoining the Birmingham Canal. When William became bedridden in 1870, John took complete control of the company. Stephen relinquished his involvement the same year. At this time the

youngest sons of William Thompson — Enoch and Samuel — set up their own rival business in the area, which developed into the firm Thompson Brothers, also well-known as a tanker manufacturer. Ironically, Thompson Brothers became part of the John Thompson Group in the 1960s.

Between 1871 and 1900 the company built boilers for ships, railway engines and power stations for use throughout the United Kingdom and, more importantly, for export around the world, allowing John Thompson's boilers to become a byword which would last throughout the history of boilermaking. Three Lancashire Boilers (as they were known) were ordered by India State Railways in 1895, when John Thompson vertical engines and boilers were being produced alongside traction engines and water tube boilers. By the 1920s and 1930s Thompson's was producing road tankers and, with profits growing at a rapid rate, in 1936 it was decided to float John Thompson as a public company. The John Thompson Engineering Co was established with a share capital of £1 million pounds. The name was shortened in 1947 to John Thompson Ltd.

With the outbreak of war in 1939 many employees were called up to serve their country and, as during

World War 1, the company was designated to build essential engineered products for the war effort. Boilers for steam gunboats, bomb containers, aircraft exhaust pipes and tank turrets were produced, together with Mulberry Harbour bridges and landing craft for D-Day.

When John Thompson, the youngest son of the original John Thompson who died in 1909, retired in 1947, technology was rapidly advancing, with much research taking place into a peaceful use for atomic energy. John Thompson Ltd was at the forefront of the research and development programme, which culminated in an order to the company for the fast-breeder reactor at Dounreay.

Thompson eventually became part of Northern Engineering Industries (NEI-Thompson was the new name) in 1968, the production of road tankers continuing to be the mainstay of the company throughout this period. The road tanker division of Thompson's was later formed out of an alliance between Thompson and Carmichael (itself founded in 1837) in 1992 and in 1998 the company — Thompson Carmichael Ltd —

was acquired by Heil Trailer International Incorporated of Tennessee, USA (which is itself a Dover Corporation subsidiary company, having being acquired in 1993), becoming part of the Heil Group, which specialises in road tankers and dust carts. Today, at Bilston in the West Midlands, Thompson-Heil Trailer International Ltd, as the British arm of the company is now known, manufactures hundreds of tankers every year for petrol distributors, food and liquid suppliers, bitumen and chemical companies and undertakes refurbishment and modification work on existing fleets.

Above:
A Thompson's airport refuelling tanker mounted on a Bedford chassis in the mid-1930s. *Ernie Flavell, Heil Trailer International*

Below:
This tank was built by Thompson's of Bilston and fitted to this truck in the mid-1930s.
Ernie Flavell, Heil Trailer International

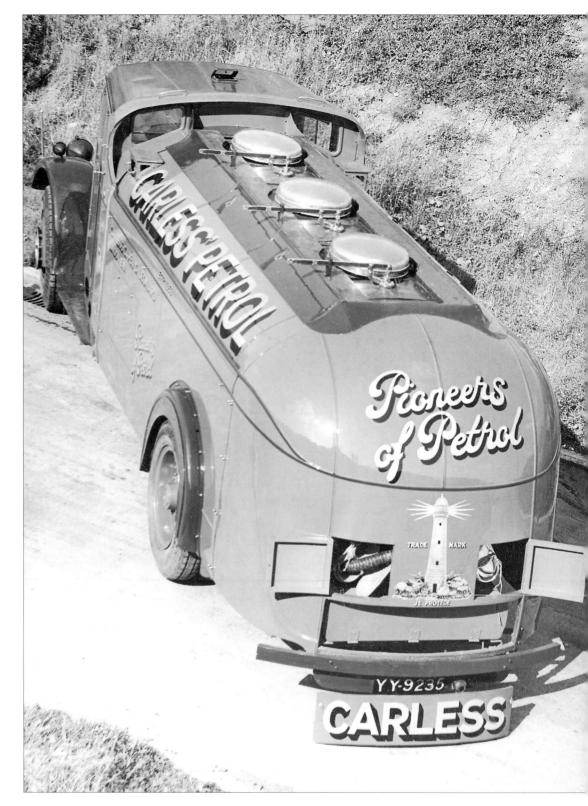

Left:
This Thompson streamline tanker was fitted to an AEC chassis in the early 1930s and operated by Carless Petrol. *Ernie Flavell, Heil Trailer International*

Top:
This 1,250-gallon five-compartment tank, built by Thompson Brothers of Bilston was, around 1933-4, mounted on a Leyland chassis. *Ernie Flavell, Heil Trailer International*

Above:
Mounted on a Fordson chassis was this 1920s Thompson's 'Sussex' refuelling unit. Many of Thompson's models were named after English counties. *Ernie Flavell, Heil Trailer International*

Right:
This time a Leyland chassis is being employed to carry this Thompson streamline aviation tanker in the mid-1930s. *Ernie Flavell, Heil Trailer International*

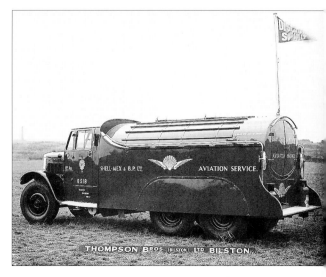

Is it a racing car? No, it is a self-propelled aviation lubricating oil dispenser. A to E were all were produced between the 1920s and the 1950s. The earliest were said to be among the first purpose-built aircraft refuelling, lubricating and servicing vehicles in regular use at that time. All were produced at Bilston by Thompson's — now Thompson-Heil Trailer International, UK. *Ernie Flavell, Heil Trailer International*

Below:
A model TB (Thompson Brothers) 'Mobile' aircraft refuelling tender, working at the RAF civil training college at Desford, Lincolnshire, during the 1930s. The aeroplanes are Tiger Moths.
Ernie Flavell, Heil Trailer International

Heil Trailer International

The original Heil company was formed in 1901 by Julius P. Heil, one of the first tanker manufacturers in the United States. In common with many of America's great pioneering industrialists, Julius came from the Old World to a Wisconsin farm with his parents. He was only 12 when he quit school to work outside the farm, then just two years later he moved to Milwaukee to work and live with his brother Frank. After trying a number of jobs he began working for Herman Falk, a young engineer and friend of Frank. Albert Hoffman, an employee of the Milwaukee Electric Railway Company, approached Falk with a process for welding street railway rails that had many advantages. Julius Heil quickly learnt the technique and found himself work in many of America's growing cities — Chicago, St Louis, New York and Washington DC, where he met President McKinley. By Herman Falk's recommendation, Heil was asked by a London engineer to take on a new challenge of a rail-welding job in Buenos Aires, which he readily accepted. Work started in 1899. By the end of that year he had gained new confidence in himself and his future. In June 1900 Julius Heil married Elizabeth Conrad and they decided to start their own business. In 1901, Julius P. Heil founded the Heil Rail Joint Company in Milwaukee, Wisconsin, pioneering the use of electric welding. As the company grew and prospered, Heil began building truck bodies, hydraulic hoists and a variety of truck trailers for the new-born automotive industry. Many orders were received for simple sheet metalwork on tanks of all shapes and sizes. With his future clearly mapped out, he changed the name of the company in 1906 to The Heil Company. By then he was making tanks for the wagon company of Charles Abresch, for the Standard Oil Company of Indiana, the Wadhams Oil Company and the O'Neil Oil and Paint company, and by the 1920s and 1930s the company had grown into one of the leading tanker manufacturers in the the United States.

Left:
A 1,200-gallon three-compartment elliptical Heil tank mounted on a 3½-ton Model 40 White truck for the Ault & Wilborg Company of New York, USA, is being used to haul printer's ink. The photograph shows the tank loading in front of The Evening Sun plant in Baltimore, Maryland. The tank is furnished complete with 14in manholes, 6in fillers, ¾in full-flow vents, adjustable sills, hinged metal can racks, a bumper, etc. The tank is fitted with a 1½in steam coil in each compartment. *Michele Harris, Heil Trailer International, USA*

Left:

In 1927 Heil introduced this 1,000-gallon milk tank — the world's first welded stainless steel tank. *Michele Harris, Heil Trailer International, USA*

Left:

This Heil 2,700-gallon semi-elliptical six-compartment truck tank, mounted on a LaPeer trailer, is hauled by a Diamond T truck. Compartments from front to back carry 250-550-550-550-550-250 gallons. The vehicle has 12in running boards, stationary 18in-high can racks open at each end, a handrail full length of the tank on each side, 14in manholes, 6in fillers, 3/4in full-flow vents, 2in piping and Wheaton faucets. The tank is 6ft wide and 15ft 2in long. It is seen here operating in the late 1920s.
Michele Harris, Heil Trailer International, USA

Above:

This is a Heil 2,400-gallon four-compartment, drop frame trailer tank, mounted on a Fruehauf trailer, hauled by a Diamond T tractor unit. Each tank compartment is fitted with a 14in manhole, 6in filler plugs, a 2in individual control emergency valve, a 2in single pipeline, and there is a special running board on top of the tank covered with aluminium sheeting. On each side are underslung can boxes and immediately below the running boards, running the entire length of the tank, are three hose compartments. The metal can box is of the integral type with a hinged door. This vehicle entered service on the 20 March 1928. *Michele Harris, Heil Trailer International, USA*

The company's global presence has continued to grow, with manufacturing facilities today in Southeast Asia, South America, North America and the UK (Thompson-Heil Trailer International Ltd). Road tankers are produced from aluminium, stainless steel and, with its 5000 Series, carbon steel. Heil can provide tankers with from one to 15 compartments, based on a tri-axle articulated design, operating at maximum capacity under current legislation.

Amongst the tankers manufactured today by Heil is the Urban Artic, a dual (two)-axle articulated road tanker, which allows operators to negotiate narrow and difficult urban areas, to reach inner-city petrol fore-courts for example. Non-tip cement tankers such as the NT44/3SS/A-A3 from Heil are built using finite element analysis (computer-aided design) and utilising a choice of discharge methods, including an on-board powerpack consisting of a Kubota engine with a GHH CG80 blower. Other Heil models include the rigid chassis ADE349 with four or five compartments containing a total of between 12,500 and 14,500 litres on two axles; the AD393 three-axle five-compartment model on a rigid chassis, and models AD367, AD349, AD393 and AD367 which are mounted on a rigid chassis of up to four axles with a maximum 26,000 litres capacity in five or six compartments.

Above:
In August 1938 this articulated trailerised milk tanker of 2,500 gallons capacity, with a single compartment, was hauled by a Model BM Mack with 12ft 1in wheelbase. The Heil tank featured a burnished aluminium outer cover. It was used by Palmer Transfer of Scranton, Pennsylvania, USA. *Michele Harris, Heil Trailer International, USA*

Left:
This 700-gallon capacity tanker was the world's first fully streamlined truck tank. It had two compartments and was built by Heil in 1933. *Michele Harris, Heil Trailer International, USA*

Below:
In 1936 Heil built the first frameless trailerised transport. It, like other earlier tankers, was of a streamline design. *Michele Harris, Heil Trailer International, USA*

Above:
A Heil tanker on an FWD chassis refuelling unit provides gas, oil, water and air in the servicing of this biplane on 8 August 1930. *Michele Harris, Heil Trailer International, USA*

Right:
The Badger Oil Company of Milwaukee, Wisconsin, used in the 1930s this 1,000-gallon Heil four-compartment elliptical tank on a Mack bus chassis with 16ft 4in wheelbase. *Michele Harris, Heil Trailer International, USA*

Below:
A 2,000-gallon capacity Heil, elliptical, four-compartment tanker on a Fruehauf trailer, seen in April 1931. The tractor is a Diamond T. *Michele Harris, Heil Trailer International, USA*

400 GALLON D/C MILD STEEL PETROL TANK & DRUM CARRIER MOUNTED ON
BEDFORD LONG WHEELBASE CHASSIS

Left:
**A Butterfields
400-gallon
tank mounted
on a Bedford
long wheelbase
chassis used in
the early
1930s.**
*Ernie Flavell,
Heil Trailer
International*

Right:
**A stainless
steel
Butterfields
tank mounted
on a 1933 AEC
chassis.**
*Ernie Flavell,
Heil Trailer
International*

STAINLESS STEEL TANK WAGGON ON A.E.C. CHASSIS
BODY WORK BY BUTTERFIELDS OF SHIPLEY

Left:
**Butterfields
supplied a
1,000-gallon
tank with
double
compartment
for use on an
Albion chassis
for this
Liverpool-
based oil
distributor in
1934.**
*Ernie Flavell, Heil
Trailer
International*

Right:
A 2,500-gallon, five-compartment tank made by Butterfields of Shipley, Yorkshire, mounted on an early 1930s Leyland Hippo chassis.
Ernie Flavell, Heil Trailer International

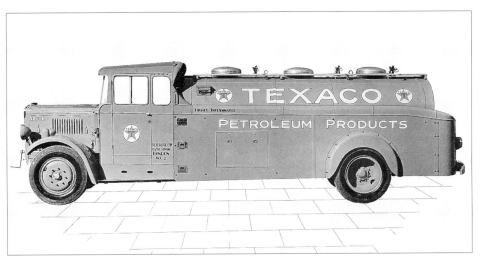

Right:
The Texas Oil Company (Texaco) purchased this road tanker incorporating a 1,500-gallon triple-compartment streamline petrol tank mounted on a Karrier 'Chaser Six' chassis around 1929.
Ernie Flavell, Heil Trailer International

Right:
A Butterfields 1,500-gallon triple-compartment, dual-purpose spirit or tar product tank on an AEC chassis in the late 1920s/ early 1930s.
Ernie Flavell, Heil Trailer International

Top:
An early Albion road tanker on test in the 1930s.
Ian Allan Library

Above:
An Albion six-cylinder heavy-duty chassis, converted as a tractor, which was operated by Aberdeen and District Milk Marketing Board. It employed this machine on the collection of milk in bulk road-rail trailers, the laden weight of which was 18 tons. The tractor was provided with a front drawbar connection so that the tanks could be pushed onto railway trucks for dispatch to the south. The photograph was taken on 12 October 1940.
Ian Allan Library

Above:
An Albion road tanker operating in the West Midlands in 1950. *Ian Allan Library*

Below:
An Albion road tanker at work on 28 June 1941 in South Africa. *Ian Allan Library*

Above:
This Thornycroft road tanker, which incorporated a five-compartment tank, was owned and operated by Distillers Ltd. The picture is dated 26 October 1935. *Ian Allan Library*

Right:
This Thornycroft 'Handy' 2-ton chassis truck has a 600-gallon, two-compartment spirit tank manufactured by the Aluminium Plant and Vessel Co Ltd of Putney, London, mounted on it. The date of the picture is 29 June 1935.
Ian Allan Library

Above:

This Butterfields 2,500-gallon, five-compartment supa-gravity tank was mounted on a Leyland Hippo chassis around 1931. Note the vehicle's speed restriction warning — 20mph.

Ernie Flavell, Heil Trailer International

Below:

Few details are available on this Butterfields streamline tanker, thought to be mounted on an early 1930s AEC chassis.

Ernie Flavell, Heil Trailer International

Above:

A 1,000-gallon petrol tanker on a 3-ton forward-control Fordson chassis on demonstration. The date is 7 May 1938. *Ian Allan Library*

Below:

An AEC Ranger from 1934 sporting a 1,500-gallon tank by Thompson Brothers of Bilston. *Ernie Flavell, Heil Trailer International*

On municipal duties is this Dennis-mounted Butterfields 1,150-gallon capacity Dennis gully emptier from the 1930s.
Ernie Flavell, Heil Trailer International

John Thornycroft built this truck which went into service complete with triple-compartment tank and refuelling hoses on 16 July 1938.
Ian Allan Library

Left:
An ERF (Edwin Richard Foden) from the early 1930s. This model was known as the CI68, working here as a road tanker throughout Lancashire.
Carl Johnson, ERF Register

Right:
From 1937, this is an ERF C1662 road tanker transporting acids for a company based in Leeds.
Carl Johnson, ERF Register

Left:
Registered in June 1937, this ERF 2CI4 was working for Wakefield Castrol; note the four-compartment tank and its four manholes, which are used both to load the vehicle, and to enable tank cleaning to be carried out efficiently.
Carl Johnson, ERF Register

Above:
This ERF CI682 was registered in January 1947. It operated as a bulk tanker from its base in Sale, Cheshire. *Carl Johnson, ERF Register*

Below:
ERF model CI682 road tanker in February 1949 working for Flitol in the Bedford area. *Carl Johnson, ERF Register*

This Commer road tanker with triple compartments was photographed on the 29 June 1940. *Ian Allan Library*

Below:
This Commer 'Superpoise' 4/5-ton milk tanker is equipped with a 1,000-gallon Butterfield stainless steel tank, and was supplied to John Fairclough of Ingleton, by Grace & Sutcliffe Ltd of Keighley in Yorkshire, seen on 5 October 1946. *Ian Allan Library*

Above:

A Dennis Pax from November 1955 with a Thompson Brother's tanker for the distribution of lubricating oils on board.
Ernie Flavell, Heil Trailer International

Below:

A Thornycroft 'Swiftsure', 800-gallon cesspit emptier with Thornycroft all-metal cab and Eagle tank and equipment, supplied to Famagusta Municipal Corporation, seen on 14 June 1958.
Ian Allan Library

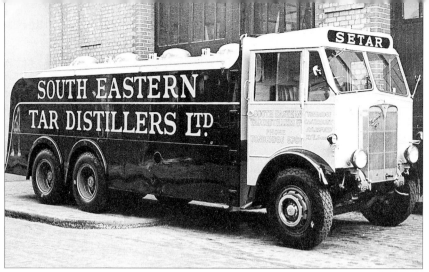

Left:
An AEC tar tanker from the 1940s operating in the southeast of England.
Ian Allan Library

Right:
An AEC Mammoth Major, operated by Harold Wood & Sons Ltd for the Shell Chemical Manufacturing Co, from its Stanlow Plant at Bromborough, Cheshire, carrying 13 tons of liquid sulphur on 3 July 1954.
Ian Allan Library

Left:
Smith and Robinson Ltd of Rothwell, Leeds, was the proud owner of this AEC Mammoth Major road tanker in 1953. The vehicle was supplied by ACV Sales Ltd of Southall, Middlesex, which also supplied buses, coaches, railcars, marine and stationary oil engines and lorries.
Ian Allan Library

In 1953/4 an AEC Mammoth Major with 1,500–gallon tank and tar spraying equipment was supplied to the Burmese Government. It was equipped with a Bonallack cab. *Ian Allan Library*

An AEC Mammoth Major was equipped with bulk cement containers for GNR. This view is dated 27 March 1954. *Ian Allan Library*

Above:
Crow Carrying Co of Barking in Essex was using this Bedford truck equipped with a 900–gallon Thompson Brothers tank on 10 May 1941.
Ian Allan Library

Below:
Built in Argentina with a Bedford 5-ton, short-wheelbase chassis as the tractor unit and with a detachable semi-trailer, this tanker carried sulphuric acid for Industrias Quimicas Argentines, South America, during the mid–1950s.
Ian Allan Library

Above:
This 28-hp Bedford OLBC was built in 1952. It had been owned by the Ministry of Defence and is thought to have been equipped to transport fuel. It was purchased in 1985 in a derelict condition, and came complete with brass dipsticks. Totally restored by its present owners, S. J. Bargh Ltd, haulage contractors of Caton, Lancaster, it is a frequent visitor to steam gatherings and vintage rallies throughout the Northwest, displayed by Bargh's warehouse manager Mr Mick Johnson. *Mick Johnson/S. J. Bargh*

Below:
A 1950s Bedford tanker employed by FINA.
Dennis Sherer, Vauxhall Motors

Right:
Seen in Swansea, in September 1957, was this Mobil oil tanker on a Bedford chassis.
R. L. Wilson

Below:
A Bedford articulated road tanker in Pickfords livery in the early 1950s.
Dennis Sherer, Vauxhall Motors

Above:
Keeping the capital's buses going was the job of this London Transport Bedford road tanker during the 1940s/early 1950s. *Dennis Sherer, Vauxhall Motors*

Below:
This Eagle gully emptier is mounted on a Bedford chassis and is working in Kent in the 1950s.
Dennis Sherer, Vauxhall Motors

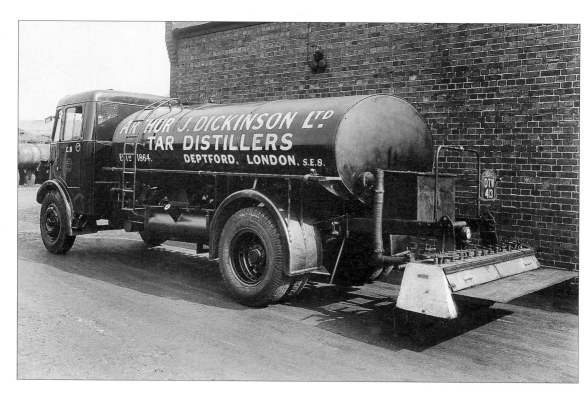

An Albion M550 fitted with a tar tank and spreading equipment supplied by Thompson Brothers and photographed on 10 May 1941.
Ian Allan Library

Below:
This 1,500-gallon tanker on an Albion CX29 10-ton chassis was photographed on 16 May 1942.
Ian Allan Library

Above:
The Commonwealth Oil Refineries Ltd of Sydney placed in service during the early 1950s this bulk oil-carrying tank wagon on an Albion 10-ton twin-steer chassis. An Albion six-cylinder direct injection oil engine gave it power. Note the unusual half-cab provided for the driver.
Ian Allan Library

Below:
A 1955 Albion Clydesdale, 1,000-gallon vacuum tanker built at Albion Motors' Scotstoun factory in Glasgow. *Ian Allan Library*

Above:
**Another Albion Clydesdale from 1955, this time
on aviation service in Brisbane, Australia.**
Ian Allan Library

Below:
**Working with a 1,000-gallon tank, this Clydesdale
from Albion was built for water transportation
duties in 1955.** *Ian Allan Library*

Above:
An Albion Caledonian 4 x 4 rigid road tanker photographed on 9 November 1957.
Ian Allan Library

Below:
This Albion Caledonian eight-wheeled chassis, with 4,000-gallon, five-compartment tank, each of which was fitted with stainless steel steam-heated coils. The whole tank is lined with Prodo-glass, and was built by the Steel Barrel Co Ltd. The completed veicle was photographed on 27 September 1958. *Ian Allan Library*

Above:
A 1940s Atkinson bulk tanker at work for Spurrier, Glazebrook and Co Ltd of Manchester. *Ian Allan Library*

Below:
The Scammell articulated bulk tanker operated by Lever Brothers Port Sunlight Ltd, undertaking deliveries in 1953. *Ian Allan Library*

Top:
In the service of Mr Therm, an impressive road tanker on a 3-ton Austin chassis put to work in June 1939 for the Sheffield & District Gas Co. W. P. Butterfield Ltd built the tank and equipment.
Ian Allan Library

Above:
An Austin rigid-chassis petrol tanker in the service of the Anglo American Oil Co in the early 1950s.
Ian Allan Library

Left:
An articulated road tanker built by ERF for export to Kingston, Jamaica. This model was known as the 649X.
Carl Johnson, ERF Register

Right:
In 1955 this ERF 689 was employed hauling oil and fuel from its Liverpool base.
Carl Johnson, ERF Register

Left:
An ERF 88R, with eight-cylinder Rolls-Royce petrol engine and disc brakes, carrying a 4,000-gallon alloy tank sometime during the late 1960s and early 1970s.
ERF Ltd/Carl Johnson, ERF Register

Above:
One of a number of Thornycroft Trusty 4 x 2 tractors with composite cabs, fifth wheel attachment and steel barrel comprising 3,200 gallons capacity, four-compartment frameless lubricating oil tank, operated by C. C Wakefield and Co Ltd. The rear end of the tank is supported on a Dyson tandem axle assembly, operating on 26 November 1955. *Ian Allan Library*

Below:
One of a number of Thornycroft road tankers operated by British Viscoleum Fuels Ltd in November 1954. This Nippy Star 1,200-gallon vehicle has a Butterfield tank and 6ft x 6ft rack to the rear end for the carriage of oil drums. The tank is of aluminium construction and the contents are discharged via a Stothert & Pitt pump. Unladen weight of the vehicle was less than 3 tons. *Ian Allan Library*

Top:
This AEC Mammoth Major was photographed on
3 March 1956. It carried a 4,000-gallon Thompson
Brothers tank comprising five 800-gallon
compartments. The gross vehicle weight was 24
tons when carrying 4,000 gallons of white spirit,
3,800 gallons of vaporising oil or 3,300 gallons of
heavy oil. *Ian Allan Library*

Above:
Another AEC Mammoth Major from the 1950s.
Ian Allan Library

Above:
This AEC Mercury was engaged in transporting grain in bulk and was seen in March 1956 working for Gilstrap, Earp Co Ltd (Maltsters) of Newark. The alloy body was built by the Duramin Engineering Co Ltd, and had two chutes fitted in the rear from which the grain was discharged.
Ian Allan Library

Below:
An AEC at work for Caltex on 24 July 1965.
Ian Allan Library

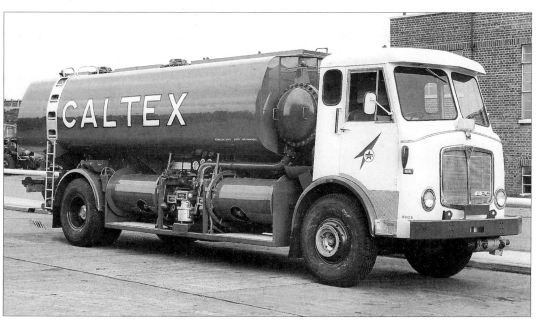

Above:
A Commer tractor hauling a bulk tanker trailer for the Shell Co in Brazil, South America. These vehicles were supplied through Companhia Brasileira de Veiculos and operated in and around Rio de Janeiro in the late 1950s. *Ian Allan Library*

Below:
A Commer milk tanker loading up from a farm in Galloway, Scotland, in 1959. *Ian Allan Library*

Left:
A Leyland Comet articulated streamline road tanker in 1957. *R. L. Wilson*

Right:
A Leyland Super Comet articulated road tanker on 4 August 1960. *R. L. Wilson*

Left:
A Bedford 4 x 4 road tanker complete with refuelling booms and hoses mounted above the tank. The date is 6 October 1959. *R. L. Wilson*

Above:

These two mighty AEC 4 x 4 bulk tankers operated from their depot in Hull around 1959/60. *Ian Allan Library*

Below:

Tunnel Cement was using an AEC tractor unit to haul this tank-like bottom dump trailer on 22 January 1966. *Ian Allan Library*

Above right:

Two AEC Mercury bulk cement carriers leaving Tunnel Cement's plant on 14 October 1957. *Ian Allan Library*

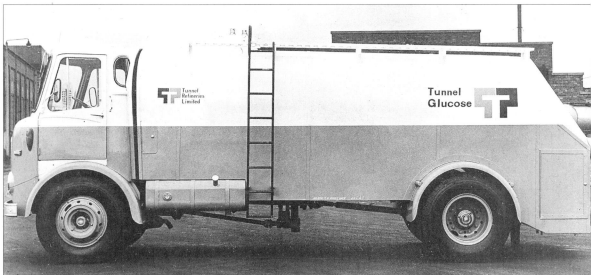

Above:

A single-compartment 1,500-gallon tank mounted on an AEC Mercury chassis. The tank was made and supplied by W. P. Butterfield (Engineers) Ltd of Shipley, Yorkshire, for James Hemphill Ltd of Glasgow. Hemphill's operated the tanker on behalf of Tunnel Refineries Ltd. The stainless steel tank is insulated with 2in thick glass fibre, whilst the insulation cladding and panelling are of aluminium. There is a small compartment at the rear of the main tank, but within the outer cladding, which houses a 4in Stothert & Pitt pump, driven from the power take-off. This vehicle is seen here at work on 16 December 1965. *Ian Allan Library*

Above:
On 14 September 1965 this AEC Mandator tractor was using a tank built by Neville Industries of Mansfield, Nottinghamshire, to move bulk powders, which are discharged with the help of twin-cylinder hydraulic rams. *Ian Allan Library*

Below:
An AEC tractor is in front of this bulk cement tanker operating for Tunnel Cement in May 1968. *Ian Allan Library*

Below:
The tanker shown carries liquefied ethylene gas in its 4,120-gallon tank built by Butterfields of Shipley. It operated between the Esso Refinery at Fawley, Hampshire and Associated Octel at Hayle, Cornwall, and Amlwch, Anglesey in North Wales. The tractor was an AEC Mandator, fitted with a 196bhp six-cylinder engine. It was photographed on 30 December 1965. *Ian Allan Library*

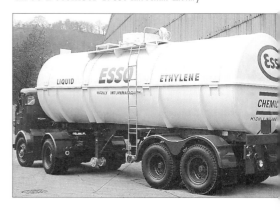

Right:
A Bedford bulk tanker being loaded with grain on 7 May 1956.
Ian Allan Library

Below:
This Bedford–Scammell bulk tanker was photographed on 30 August 1952.
Ian Allan Library

Above:
A pair of Bedford bulk road tankers with streamline articulated tanks loading from the Coryton Refinery. Petrol, derv fuel and gas oil were available from this depot. A shuttle service of road tank wagons deliver fuels from the bulk terminal situated outside the refinery area near the Cory Institute.

The two tankers shown have capacities of 2,400 gallons each. The flow meter — introduced to the United Kingdom for the first time by the Vacuum Oil Co to replace the old method of checking delivery by dipstick — is housed behind the small doors seen beneath the word Mobilgas on the side of the vehicle tanks. Thought to be around 1958/9. *Ian Allan Library*

Left:
This Bedford articulated tanker was being used to transport liquid egg, on 23 July 1960.
Ian Allan Library

Above:
British Railways used this Bedford truck to move a demountable pressurised container for the movement of powdered starch in bulk from Messrs Brown & Polson Ltd of Paisley in Scotland to Birmingham on this occasion on 23 March 1962. Naturally, the main journey will have been undertaken by rail. *Ian Allan Library*

Below:
Two Bedford airport refuelling tankers from the 1960s in Singapore. *Dennis Sherer, Vauxhall Motors*

Above:
Bedford articulated tar tankers parked up in the late 1950s/early 1960s. *Dennis Sherer, Vauxhall Motors*

Below:
An aircraft servicing tanker on a Bedford chassis in the late 1950s/early 1960s.
Dennis Sherer, Vauxhall Motors

Above:
A British Oxygen Co gas tanker on a Bedford chassis in the 1950s. *Dennis Sherer, Vauxhall Motors*

Below:
During the late 1950s/early 1960s, this Bedford-mounted 4 x 4 rigid-chassis road tanker was working out of Luton, Bedfordshire.
Dennis Sherer, Vauxhall Motors

Top:
A Bedford road tanker from the late 1950s/early 1960s. *Dennis Sherer, Vauxhall Motors*

Above:
In Swansea in September 1957 was this Bedford Mobil oil tanker. *R. L. Wilson*

Left:
Working in Switzerland in the 1960s was this Bedford-mounted road tanker and its single-axle tank trailer. *Dennis Sherer, Vauxhall Motors*

Below:
On this earthmoving project the hungry bulldozers and scrapers are refuelled via a Bedford-mounted tanker working for the contractor John Laing. *Dennis Sherer, Vauxhall Motors*

Left:
**This Thompson
Brothers tank and
associated equipment is
mounted on a Bedford
chassis from the late
1950s/early 1960s.**
*Dennis Sherer, Vauxhall
Motors*

Right:
**A Bedford rigid-chassis
road tanker seen in
London.**
*Dennis Sherer, Vauxhall
Motors*

Left:
**A Bedford-mounted
tanker with refuelling
boom, pipes, pumps
and equipment in the
early 1960s.**
*Dennis Sherer, Vauxhall
Motors*

Above:
An AEC Mammoth Major 8, with 3,000-gallon insulated tank on a pub run on 23 December 1961 — just in time for the Christmas rush! *Ian Allan Library*

Below:
This AEC Mandator was photographed at Southampton Docks on 10 July 1965. It and a similar vehicle alongside are unloading a cargo of wine from the *Southampton Castle* to their huge articulated tankers, which carry around 4000 gallons each. *Ian Allan Library*

Right:
An AEC Mandator articulated road tanker (gross vehicle weight 16 tons) carrying 10½ tons of liquid ammonia. The photograph was taken in 1968.
Ian Allan Library

Right:
In 1968 an AEC Mandator tractor and its bulk tanker pose for a photograph at this well-known brewery.
Ian Allan Library

Right:
An AEC road tanker doing what it does best, gobbling up mile after mile of motorway en route to its destination in the late 1960s.
Ian Allan Library

Left:
One of 15 24-ton-capacity bulk flour carriers featuring the AEC Mammoth Major 8 in 1969/70.
Ian Allan Library

Above:
Transporting liquid sulphur in 1964 with an AEC tractor and an insulated tanker trailer fitted with heating coils to maintain the correct temperature for the cargo on board. *Ian Allan Library*

Below:
Two AEC Mandators hauling bulk tankers with cargoes of flour on board, around 1971.
Ian Allan Library

Above:
A 1965 AEC Mandator with Bonallack light alloy tank with air discharge to assist unloading its cargo of cement. The picture was taken on 22 January 1966 at the Tunnel Cement works. *Ian Allan Library*

Below:
This AEC Mammoth Major with massive 8,290-gallon tank has a total length of 47ft. The gross vehicle weight is 40 ton and it operated in Australia from June 1967. *Ian Allan Library*

Above:
Bulk flour on the move in May 1968 aboard this mighty 4 x 4 road tanker.
Ian Allan Library

Right:
A Bedford TK takes charge of this trailerised tipping tanker in May 1968. Kaolin is powdered china clay.
Ian Allan Library

Below:
A Foden tractor unit with a bulk powder tank by Crane Fruehauf, operating in the Northwest of England in May 1968. *Ian Allan Library*

Top:
**An Atkinson provides the power to haul this hefty
bulk powder tanker, seen in May 1968.**
Ian Allan Library

Above:
**Another Atkinson tractor hauling fuel oil, again in
May 1968.** *Ian Allan Library*

Top:
An ERF with a Thompson tanker in the livery of The National Oil Co, during the late 1960s/early 1970s. *Ernie Flavell, Heil Trailer International*

Above:
Thompson Brothers of Bilston supplied the tank and associated equipment, whilst ERF supplied this turbo truck and chassis in the 1970s.
Ernie Flavell, Heil Trailer International

Right:
An ERF LAC (LV A series Cummins engine) working for world-famous haulier Pickfords in 1974. *Carl Johnson, ERF Register*

Above:
A Leyland tractor unit hauling this mighty fuel tanker in May 1968. *Ian Allan Library*

Left:
Leyland lorries are being used to transport these pressure vessels from Harland and Wolff's yard in Belfast, where they were manufactured in January 1968. *Ian Allan Library*

Below:
The Crow Carrying Co was using this Crane Fruehauf–built bulk tanker in May 1968.
Ian Allan Library

Bottom:
A Leyland tractor coupled to a 4,000-gallon tank in January 1968. *Ian Allan Library*

Above:

Refuelling a Vickers–Armstrong Valiant at Farnborough in 1955; this Leyland chassis carries all the equipment required to service such an aircraft for the RAF.

Ernie Flavell, Heil Trailer International

Below:

Eight aircraft refuelling tankers with on-board compressors for air supply, tanks for fuel, water, etc, photographed during the 1970s. *Ernie Flavell, Heil Trailer International*

Top:
During the early 1960s, a Bedford refuels a DH114 Heron at Newcastle Airport.
Dennis Sherer, Vauxhall Motors

Above:
A Seddon-Atkinson truck/chassis refuelling this Handley Page Herald from a Thompson tank and equipment, probably during the 1970s.
Ernie Flavell, Heil Trailer International

Right:
A Seddon-Atkinson tractor and a Thompson aircraft refuelling tanker sometime in the early 1990s.
Ernie Flavell, Heil Trailer International

Above:

The tank on this AEC Mammoth Major had a capacity of 4,500 gallons and carried liquid butane. It was built by G. A. Harvey and was photographed on 19 October 1963. *Ian Allan Library*

Below:

A D–Series Ford with its tanker cargo of LPG (liquefied petroleum gas). *Ian Allan Library*

Above:
A Leyland chassis and triple-compartment tank and enclosed metering, pumping and associated equipment mounted at the rear end of the tank, all built and supplied by Thompson Brothers of Bilston.
Ernie Flavell, Heil Trailer International

Right:
In 1984 this Bedford was used to carry a Thompson-built tank, fitted with totally enclosed hose and pumping gear at the rear end.
Ernie Flavell, Heil Trailer International

Left:
A Dodge chassis and Thompson tank ready for work in the 1980s.
Ernie Flavell, Heil Trailer International

Above:

A Leyland in 1975 on its way to work with a Thompson tank and equipment.
Ernie Flavell, Heil Trailer International

Right:

A Leyland Freighter chassis with Thompson tanker on fuel/oil/petrol duties in the early 1980s.
Ernie Flavell, Heil Trailer International

Below:

The Crane Fruehauf tanker in this photograph was rated at 38 tonnes. It used a tri-axle trailer drawn by a Leyland tractor, and worked for Minster Transport Ltd of Wimborne, Dorset, in 1984. *Ian Allan Library*

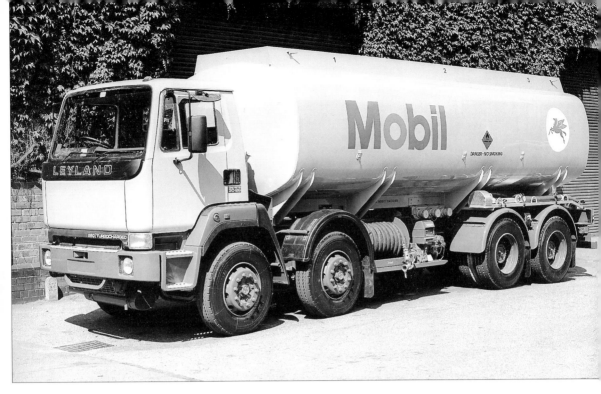

Above:

A Leyland turbocharged 260 chassis carried this triple-compartment Thompson tank in the 1980s.
Ernie Flavell, Heil Trailer International

Below:

This Leyland Constructor water tanker is seen at work on Malta in the 1990s. *Tony Brown*

Left:
A Bedford TK, with on-board Whale tank and gully-emptying boom, pump and hoses, ready to go to work in the early 1970s.
Julian Fishwick, Whale Tankers Ltd

Whale Tankers

Although the history of this company is relatively recent, its success has been unrivalled. From the conversion of an 'old' Series 1 Land-Rover being fitted with a Vee-8 engine, before such conversions became a fashionable ploy by those with motor engineering skills, the three gentlemen behind this escapade went on to form a highly successful manufacturing company of municipal and industrial road tankers, with export achievements which match the vehicles' popularity on British soil.

In 1969, Mike Fisher, Keith Palmer and John Browne formed a company called Fusion (Beckinhill) Ltd, each contributing £400 towards the cost of a Land-Rover and welding set to do repairs for contractors building the Midland motorway network. Apart from the odd few pounds which came in periodically, the £1,200 was the only direct investment made in the company in the early days. Mobile welding work was found by Keith Palmer, who devoted his spare time to selling the service. Mike Fisher and John Browne got on with the work, with their first employee-shareholder, Roger Chandler, doing most of the welding. At the time, Mike, who was the son of the economist, farmer and founder of Buxted Chickens — Sir Anthony Fisher — was attached to the development department at Land-Rover, developing his SMOMOT (Specialist Machine, One Man, One Team) for use with the company's proposed forward-control vehicle. John Browne, later to become Lord Kilmain, was an

apprentice at Land-Rover and Keith Palmer, a friend of Mike Fisher and a partner in an earlier enterprise making coffee tables, was looking for some diversification. Experiments were continued with other vehicles, including a Mercedes-Benz 'Unimog' and the manufacture of a tractor-loader named the Farmhand.

The Unimog converted into a SMOMOT, complete with a silage cutter mounted in front of the triple-axle vehicle, which could load the large trailer mounted on the chassis of the vehicle. Orders arrived from Scotland and from Russia in December 1969 following a successful stand at the Smithfield Show in London, where the Unimog was given star status. This success led the company to seek out premises for a new factory and an old mill in Ravenshaw Lane, near Solihull in the West Midlands, became the solution.

With the welding business already booming, in 1970 the three partners' friend Brian Newsome finally persuaded them, after several failed attempts, that they should go into production building vacuum tankers. After buying an old disused tanker from Wellingborough Council, the idea took off in earnest. The first order came in for two 1,500-gallon vacuum tankers from Frank Taylor, who had set up his own business — Progressive Waste Disposal. With help from a friendly local bank manager and the inevitable accountant, the business was getting more than a little serious.

In 1974 a new name was adopted for the company — Whale Tankers. Vacuum tankers were to be the bread-and-butter products of the business. Indeed, with one order for 50 tanker units from the Hyundai Motor Co in Korea, and the setting up of its own tanker-hire business, known as Dasselt Hire Ltd, the future looked good. Sir Douglas Bader, the Battle of Britain's most famous war ace, was invited to officially open the company's new factory in 1981 and although the recession of the 1980s made life harder for a while, the company rode out the storm. From the early 1980s the tanker-hire division took on a new identity, using the name Whale Tanker Hire, and by the late 1990s giant tankers mounted on eight-wheel chassis, known as the KiloWhale, were being built.

Tankers are currently being built to a full 44-tonne gvw by Whale, along with such innovative machines as the Jetvac, which can clean out whole pipelines and gullies in an effort to prevent flooding and overspill into roads and property.

Above:
A Ford chassis and a Whale tank, boom, pump and associated equipment in use in the 1970s.
Julian Fishwick, Whale Tankers Ltd

Left:
A Whale gully-emptying tanker on a Leyland Boxer chassis, preventing flooding problems in Newton Abbot during the early 1970s.
Julian Fishwick, Whale Tankers Ltd

Above:
A Whale vacuum tanker on a Leyland Clydesdale chassis in the late 1970s.
Julian Fishwick, Whale Tankers Ltd

Below:
A Whale gully emptier from the mid–1970s on a Ford D-Series chassis, working for the Borough of Wellingborough. *Julian Fishwick, Whale Tankers Ltd*

Left:
**An ERF EC11
on BOC Gases
duties.**
*ERF Ltd/BOC
Gases*

Right:
**An ERF ES6 working in rural
Devon delivering oil.**
ERF Ltd/Oil Sure

Left:
**An ERF EC11
chassis on road
tanker duties.**
*ERF Ltd/British
Fuels Ltd*

Left:
Moving mountains of chalk from Melton in East Yorkshire is the task of these ERF EC11, 380hp mid-lift tractors, with either slurry tanks, bulk powder or curtain-sided platform trailers to deliver the company's products all over the UK. *ERF Ltd/Omya Croxton & Garry*

Right:
Here an ERF demonstrates its front and rear steering capability. *ERF Ltd/Total Butler Oils*

Left:
This ERF, thought to be a Model 54G from 1966 (five-cylinder, 4-wheel Gardner engine) is seen carrying corn products in its bulk tank. *Carl Johnson, ERF Register*

Right:
A 1950s Albion transporting liquid oxygen for the British Oxygen Co.
J. A. Ostle/Sue McGoldrick, BOC Gases

Right:
BOC used this Scammell articulated road tanker to deliver liquid oxygen during the 1950s/early 1960s.
J. A. Ostle/Sue McGoldrick, BOC Gases

Right:
A spherical tank from the 1940s on a mid–1960s chassis.
J. A. Ostle/Sue McGoldrick, BOC Gases

Left:
This Albion CD21 vacuum-insulated tank with a submerged hydraulic pumping system operated for BOC Gases during the 1960s.
J. A. Ostle/Sue McGoldrick, BOC Gases

Right:
A BOC Gases Foden S21 articulated road tanker from the late 1960s. *J. A. Ostle/ Sue McGoldrick, BOC Gases*

Left:
One of 10 BOC Gases tankers thus painted in 1986 to celebrate 100 years of trading.
J. A. Ostle/ Sue McGoldrick, BOC Gases

Left:
A liquid C02 tanker in the 1990s. The tank is totally insulated with stainless steel inner vessel and outward cladding.
J. A. Ostle/Sue McGoldrick, BOC Gases

Right:
This rather unusual tanker has 12 jumbo tubes carrying hydrogen within its main tank. The payload itself is only around 350kg in a vehicle of 40,000kg, gvw — such is the nature of the compressed gas. A 1996 ERF EC11 tractor unit is used to haul the articulated tanker trailer.
J. A. Ostle/Sue McGoldrick, BOC Gases

Left:
A 7½-ton Leyland DAF Mini-tanker in Cryospeed Cryogenic service in 1993.
J. A. Ostle/Sue McGoldrick, BOC Gases

Above:

A Scammell tractor with Thompson-built tanker trailer in the 1970s.

Ernie Flavell, Heil Trailer International

Below:

Scammell and Thompson mate up again in 1971.

Ernie Flavell, Heil Trailer International

Above:

Seddon–Atkinson and Thompson tankers in convoy in 1978. *Ernie Flavell, Heil Trailer International*

Below:

An Atkinson Defender tractor working with a demountable tank being unloaded by a Cole's mobile crane sometime during the 1980s. *Tony Brown, St Helens*

Above:

A 1980s Volvo F7 with an aircraft refuelling tanker. *Ernie Flavell, Heil Trailer International*

Right:

A Volvo FL10 articulated road tanker with a sulphuric acid cargo, seen in the 1990s. *Tony Brown*

Below:

A Volvo F725 rigid–chassis road tanker with Thompson equipment in 1984. *Ernie Flavell, Heil Trailer International*

Top:
This 1950s articulated road tanker with its single manhole on the tank was used by Guinness to distribute bulk loads.
Sue Garland / Guinness Archive

Above:
There is some strength behind that 1960s Bedford TK tractor unit and its tanker full of Guinness.
Sue Garland / Guinness Archive

Right:
A Leyland Marathon tractor from the mid-1970s hauling a tanker full of Guinness.
Sue Garland / Guinness Archive

Top:
A Bedford TK provides the chassis for a Thompson tank, hoses, pumps, meters and associated equipment in 1976.
Ernie Flavell, Heil Trailer International

Above:
Another Bedford TK with a Thompson tank and equipment, this time in the 1960s/early 1970s.
Ernie Flavell, Heil Trailer International

Above:
This heavy-duty Bedford 4 x 4 truck tanker was the main refuelling vehicle for contractors' equipment working in opencast mines, quarries or on construction sites.
Dennis Sherer, Vauxhall Motors

Right:
A Bedford road tanker at work in the late 1970s/early 1980s.
Dennis Sherer, Vauxhall Motors

Below:
A Bedford rigid-chassis road tanker from the 1970s, more than likely still at work in the 2000/2001 period.
Dennis Sherer, Vauxhall Motors

Above:
**An ERF E10 articulated road tanker during the
1980s/early 1990s.** *ERF Ltd*

Below:
**An ERF E10 tractor unit hauling a bitumen tank
in Malta in the 1990s.** *Tony Brown*

Right:
A Leyland DAF Cruiser rigid-chassis water tanker on Malta in the late 1990s.
Tony Brown

Right:
A Seddon–Atkinson water carrier also on Malta in the 1990s.
Tony Brown

Right:
An ERF supplying fuel throughout Malta in the 1990s.
Tony Brown

Above:

One of the largest and most notable tanker transport companies has undergone a number of name changes over the years, although its livery has barely changed. Under the Linkman name, this Foden 3325 tractor is used to haul a tri-axle multi-compartment tanker trailer in the 1980s/early 1990s. *Elizabeth O'Connor, Peter Sawell & Partners Ltd*

Above:

This ERF EC10 tractor is hauling a 16,000-litre tanker during the mid-1990s for Linkman, part of TDG Logistics. *Elizabeth O'Connor, Peter Sawell & Partners Ltd*

Left:

This tri-axle articulated road tanker hauled by an ERF E10 was employed by Nexus, the second name adopted by the TDG Group during the 1980s. *Elizabeth O'Connor, Peter Sawell & Partners Ltd*

Left:
A Volvo tractor is being used to haul this tri-axle, multi-compartment articulated road tanker for TDG Linkman in the late 1990s.
Elizabeth O'Connor, Peter Sawell & Partners Ltd

Right:
A Volvo FH12 tractor on turnaround with this Metalaire–Filliat tri-axle single compartment tanker in the late 1980s/early 1990s.
Elizabeth O'Connor, Peter Sawell & Partners Ltd

Below:
This time, TDG Logistics with an ERF EC11 and a Metalair–Filliat single compartment, tri-axle tanker at work in the 1990s.
Elizabeth O'Connor, Peter Sawell & Partners Ltd

Right:
A Volvo FL7 rigid chassis road tanker on fuel supplies on Malta during the 1990s.
Tony Brown

Below:
A Scania 113M/320 tractor hauling a massive tri-axle petrol tanker, built by Thompson–Heil of Bilston.
Ernie Flavell, Heil Trailer International

Bottom:
A DAF articulated double-axle petrol tanker built by Thompson's, at work for contractors Vallance of Heathfield near Newton Abbot in Devon in the early 1990s.
Ernie Flavell, Heil Trailer International

Right:
A Leyland Comet 16–16 chassis with Thompson tank and equipment in the mid–1990s.
Ernie Flavell, Heil Trailer International

Above:
The chassis may be either Commer/Dodge or Renault, but the tank is definitely by Thompson and from the early 1990s.
Ernie Flavell, Heil Trailer International

Right:
A Seddon-Atkinson rigid-chassis Thompson tanker in the late 1980s/early 1990s.
Ernie Flavell, Heil Trailer International

Above:
A Thompson Carmichael 5000 Series lightweight spirit tank, behind a DAF tractor in the early 1990s.
Ernie Flavell, Heil Trailer International

Right:
A Seddon-Atkinson 200 with a complete array of tanker, pumping equipment, meters and hoses in the early 1980s. The tank and equipment were built by Thompson.
Ernie Flavell, Heil Trailer International

Left:
An ERF EC11 articulated tri-axle road tanker in familiar livery, carrying petrol to garage forecourts in the 1990s.
Alison Hall, ERF Ltd

Right:
An ERF EC14 articulated road tanker working for Albright and Wilson Ltd of Widnes, Cheshire, in the 1980s/early 1990s with a Clayton Commercials multi-compartment tank.
Peter Norris, Clayton Commercials Ltd

Above:
A Mercedes-Benz tractor and tri-axle Clayton Commercials tanker on liquid chlorine duties for Sutton's Transport under contract to ICI Chemicals during the early 1990s.
Michael Sutton, Sutton's Transport

Right:
Sutton and Sons Ltd of St Helens used this ERF rigid-chassis tanker with Clayton tank unit to haul ICI solvents throughout the North of England during the early 1990s.
Michael Sutton, Sutton Transport

Clayton Commercials

Clayton Commercials Ltd's factory, at Burscough, near Wigan, is currently producing a range of tankers up to the massive tri-axle 40+ton gross vehicle weight for products ranging from petroleum and oil, foods and chemicals, to dry powders, including cement, china clay, flour, grain, stone powder, etc. Many companies involved in tanker haulage have regularly returned to Clayton's for repeat orders. Some insist on using only Clayton tankers. Facilities are also available for the refurbishment and modernisation of existing tankers, and indeed tanker fleets.

Above:
Two Scania 113m tractors with Clayton Commercials tankers engaged in hauling chemicals during the early 1990s.
Peter Norris, Clayton Commercials Ltd

Left:
A Foden 4320 tractor in the livery of Sutton's of St Helens hauling a Clayton Commercials tri-axle, multi-compartment articulated tanker trailer in the 1990s.
Peter Norris, Clayton Commercials Ltd

Left:
A Clayton 8 x 8 rigid-chassis road tanker.
Peter Norris, Clayton Commercials Ltd

Left:
An ERF 180 with a Gardner diesel and rigid chassis, transporting hydrochloric acid in the 1970s/early 1980s, for contractors Sutton's.
Tony Brown/ Sutton Transport

Left:
An ERF 180 Gardner-powered articulated tanker on sodium hydrochlorite duties for Suttons in 1973-4.
Tony Brown/ Sutton Transport

Right:
An ERF E14 on contract from Sutton's to Albright and Wilson of Widnes, Cheshire, in the early 1990s.
Tony Brown/ Sutton Transport

Left:
Another view of a Sutton's tri-axle articulated road tanker with Foden 4320 tractor, under contract to ICI.
Tony Brown/Sutton Transport

Below:
A Sutton's flat-bed articulated tri-axle trailer carrying one of many demountable tanks currently in use. These can be transported by road, rail, sea and in some cases by air. Only a crane or heavy-duty fork-lift truck is required to load or unload it.
Tony Brown/Sutton Transport

Right:
An ERF tractor pulling a Clayton tri-axle multi-compartment tank in the early to mid-1990s.
Peter Norris/Clayton Commercials Ltd

Left:
A Guy tractor and Clayton dual-axle tanker trailer in the early 1970s.
Peter Norris/Clayton Commercials Ltd

Right:
Seddon-Atkinson provided this rigid chassis for the Clayton tank and associated equipment in the early 1970s.
Peter Norris/Clayton Commercials Ltd

A selection of road tankers, manufactured by Clayton Commercials: A tri-axle articulated bulk tanker in the late 1990s/2000.
Peter Norris/Clayton Commercials Ltd

Working for hauliers Shanks and McEwan in the 1990s is this Clayton tri-axle road tanker.
Peter Norris/Clayton Commercials Ltd

Above:

Looking from the back of a Clayton dual-axle tanker trailer in the late 1990s.

Peter Norris / Clayton Commercials Ltd

Below:

A Clayton tri-axle tanker in the livery of James Lynch and Sons of Cheshire, seen during the 1990s. *Peter Norris / Clayton Commercials Ltd*

Above:

Note the rear wheel steer capabilities on this late 1990s Clayton dual-axle tanker trailer.

Peter Norris/Clayton Commercials Ltd

Below:

One of many Sutton tri-axle articulated road tankers on our motorways — all of them use Clayton-built tanks.

Peter Norris/Clayton Commercials Ltd

Above:
This early 1990s single–axle Clayton tanker trailer is in service for a cheese supplier.
Peter Norris/Clayton Commercials Ltd

Below:
A Clayton bulk powder tanker in the tip position.
Peter Norris/Clayton Commercials Ltd

Top:
An ERF E10 in the late 1980s/early 1990s with Clayton tri-axle tanker trailer.
Peter Norris/Clayton Commercials Ltd

Above:
UK Waste uses this Clayton tri-axle articulated road tanker to transport hazardous or toxic waste water, effluent and sludge to specially constructed units for disposal. *Peter Norris/Clayton Commercials Ltd*